A New True Book

SOLAR ENERGY AT WORK

By David Petersen

CHILDRENS PRESS™

CHICAGO

Solar house in Acton, Massachusetts

Library of Congress Cataloging in Publication Data

Petersen, David.
  Solar energy.

  (A New true book)
  Includes index
  Summary: Briefly describes past and present uses of solar energy, especially for heating and electricity. Includes instructions for three simple experiments and a glossary.
    1. Solar energy—Juvenile literature. [1.   Solar energy.   2.   Solar energy—Experiments.   3.   Experiments]
I. Title.
TJ810.3.P48   1985   621.47   84-23208
ISBN 0-516-01942-2   AACR2

TABLE OF CONTENTS

4

THE FRIENDLY OLD SUN

All life on the earth depends on the sun's light, warmth, and invisible energy. Without the sun, the earth would be a cold, dark, dead planet.

Without our friend the sun, there would be no animals, no trees, and no flowers. In fact, without the sun, there would be no people!

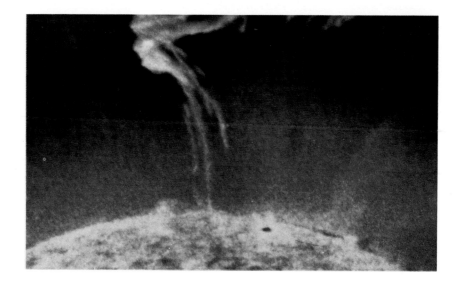

The sun is a huge ball
of burning gases. It is so
far away from the earth
that the distance is hard
to imagine—93 *million* miles!

But light from the sun
travels so fast that even at
that great distance, it takes
only eight minutes for it to
reach the earth.

WHAT IS SOLAR ENERGY?

The word *solar* comes from the Latin word *solaris,* which means sun. So *solar energy* means energy that comes from the sun.

There are many kinds of solar energy. Two of the most important are light and heat.

By using special minerals that are sensitive

In 1981 the *Solar Challenger,* powered only by solar cells on its wings, flew across the English Channel.

to sunlight, we can create solar electricity.

There are many good reasons to learn about and use solar energy. It is safe, clean, free, and as reliable as day and night!

PUTTING THE SUN
TO WORK FOR US

Solar energy is becoming more important every day.

That's because supplies of other sources of natural energy—such as gas, coal, and oil—are running out. The other form of energy, called nuclear, is probably too dangerous and expensive to rely on.

Solar energy is cheaper and safer than any other fuel. And unless the sun quits shining, we will never run out of solar energy!

This home in New Mexico is heated comfortably by solar drums in the living room and self-closing "sky-lids" in the kitchen.

SOLAR ENERGY IS NOT NEW

Many ancient peoples
used solar energy for heat.
The Egyptians, the
Greeks, the Romans, and
American Indians used the
sun to warm their homes
thousands of years ago!

The American Indians watched the sun. They saw that the winter sun was different from the summer sun. It was more to the south. They could see that in winter the warm afternoon sun was always in the western sky.

So, they decided the best direction to face a home to be warmed by the winter sun is southwest. They were right!

Remains of two early solar heating systems (above) can be seen today in Mesa Verde National Park, near Cortez, Colorado. Below, a picture of a home in the ancient city of Pompeii, Italy, shows how the sun was used for light and heat.

By the early 1900s, solar heating was very popular in America, especially in the sunny states of California and Florida.

Back then, many people used the sun to help warm their homes and to heat water.

Then natural gas was introduced as a new form of energy. Gas was so cheap and easy to use that it replaced solar energy for heating.

But today, supplies of natural gas are running out. The world does not have enough natural gas to last forever. So people are beginning to look to the sun again for heat and energy.

HEATING WITH THE SUN

When the sun's rays shine on an object, they are either absorbed by the object or reflected away from it.

Dark, dull surfaces absorb the sun's rays and become heated. The metal of a black car is a good example of an absorptive surface.

"Solar One" near Dagett, California, the world's largest solar thermal power plant, has 1,818 solar reflectors (heliostats) that focus sunlight onto a central receiver tower.

Shiny, light-colored surfaces reflect the sun's rays and stay cooler than do dark objects. The shiny side of aluminum foil is a good example of a reflective material.

Passive solar panels (bottom) and active solar panels (opposite page) collect the sun's heat. A zoo in Minneapolis (above) also makes use of solar energy.

To collect warmth from
the sun, people mount
large, flat boxes on the
roofs of their houses.
These boxes are painted
dull black. They are called
solar collectors because
they collect the sun's heat.

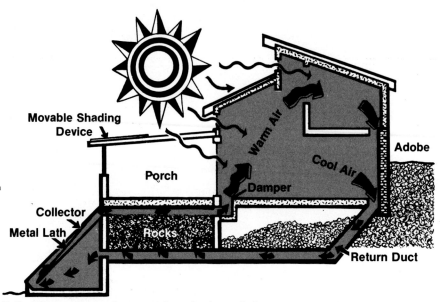

Movable Shading
Device

Adobe

Warm Air

Cool Air

Porch

Damper

Collector

Metal Lath

Rocks

Return Duct

Follow the arrows and you see how the heated air or water can rise from the solar collector and move through the solar system.

A solar collector is usually hollow and contains either air or water.

After the air or water is heated by the sun, it is moved from the collector into the house, where it can be used.

Solar Energy

Flat-Plate Collector

Cool Liquid

Heated Liquid

Heated Air

2nd Heat Element

Pump

Heat Exchanger

Pump

Blower

Water Storage

If the heated air or water moves only by gravity or other natural forces, it is called a passive solar system.

If pumps or other mechanical devices are used to help move the heated air or water, it is called an active solar system.

EXPERIMENTS YOU CAN DO

There are several easy ways to test the light-dark rule of solar heating.

Experiment 1: On a warm, sunny day, find a shiny white or silver car. Touch it to feel how warm the metal is.

Then find a car with black paint and touch it.

See how much warmer the black car is? That's because dark colors absorb the sun's heat, while light colors bounce it back into the sky.

But be careful with this experiment: On a very hot day, touching a black car could burn your hand. Remember, the sun is a very good heater!

Experiment 2: For this experiment you'll need a piece of aluminum foil about a foot square and a piece of black construction paper the same size. You'll also need an outdoor thermometer.

Go outside on a warm day, and lay the foil on the ground where it will get plenty of sunlight. The shiny side of the foil should be facing up.

Now place the thermometer under the foil. Wait at least ten minutes, then check the temperature on the thermometer. Write the number down so you won't forget it.

Now place the piece of black paper on the ground where the foil was. Put the thermometer under the black paper. Wait another ten minutes, then check the temperature again.

The temperature under the black paper is higher than under the foil! That's because a dull black surface absorbs heat better than a light-colored, shiny surface does.

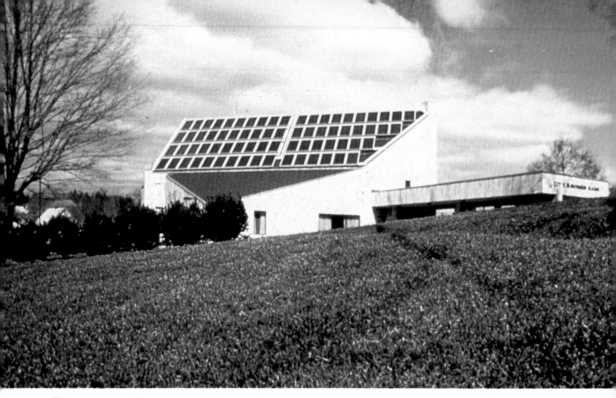

The sun supplies energy to heat the water systems
at a bank (above) and a high school (below).

SOLAR WATER HEATING

One of the most popular ways of using the sun's energy today is for heating water.

Solar collectors are placed on the roofs of houses to catch the sun's heat. These solar collectors are filled with water.

The sun-heated water is then piped down to be used in the houses. Sun-heated water is even used to warm swimming pools!

EXPERIMENT

Experiment: Find two empty cans like those soup comes in. Peel off the paper labels and wash the cans.

Paint the outside of one can dull black. If you have no black paint, cut out a piece of black construction paper, wrap it snugly around the can, and fasten it with tape.

Fill both cans with water and place them outside in the sun. While you're waiting for the sun to heat the water, ask your parents or teacher for an oral thermometer, the kind used to take temperatures.

When the cans of water have been in the sun for about an hour, dip the oral thermometer into the shiny can for a minute, and record the temperature of the water.

Then shake the thermometer and dip it into the black can for a minute. See how much warmer the water in the black can is? The solar heat absorbed by the black can warmed the water.

GREENHOUSES

Warm air is lighter in weight than cool air, so it rises. When an object is heated by the sun, some of the heat will escape by rising into the air.

A building with a clear roof will let sunshine in

Greenhouse rooms attached to the front of this house help trap and store the sun's heat.

and, at the same time, keep the rising heat from escaping. Such a building with a clear roof is called a greenhouse.

Greenhouses are used to keep plants warm in winter and to protect young plants from bad weather.

The wall at the back of this large greenhouse is made of hard packed earth. It absorbs the sun's heat during the day and slowly releases it to help keep plants warm at night.

Sunlight passes through the clear roof of a greenhouse to warm and nourish the plants inside. But when the heat tries to rise and escape, the clear roof holds it in.

ELECTRICITY FROM THE SUN

In the 1950s, scientists found a way to make electricity from the sun's energy. They called the process of making solar electricity photovoltaics.

To make electricity this way, special metal boxes, called photovoltaic panels, are placed in the sun. Often the panels are mounted atop buildings.

Sunlight striking silicon wafers in a solar module generates an electric current.

Each panel contains
many small solar cells.
These cells are round, like
cookies.

The solar cells are made
of a mineral called silicon.

Large solar panels of photovoltaic cells near Nesperih,
California, create electric power for one hundred people.

Silicon is found in sand, and can turn sunlight into electricity.

The electricity made by these silicon "cookies" is sent through wires to be stored in batteries.

WHAT HAVE WE LEARNED?

Let's review what we have learned about solar energy on earth:

- Dull, dark objects absorb the sun's energy, and get hot.

- The sun's heat "bounces off" shiny, light-colored objects, so they stay cooler.

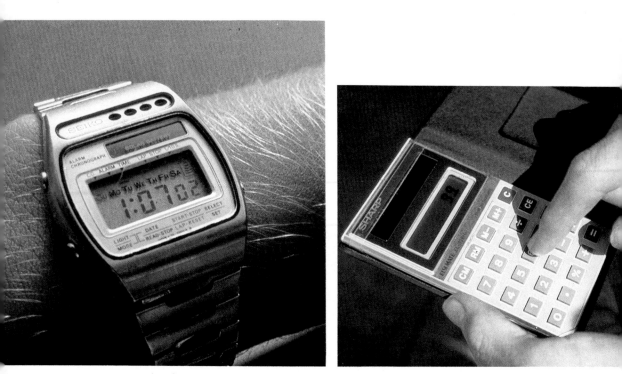

A solar watch (left) and a solar-powered calculator are among many new products sold today.

- Water can be heated by putting it in a dull black container and placing the container in the sun.
- If mechanical devices such as pumps are used

to move solar-heated air or water, it is said to be an active system.

• If no mechanical devices are used in a solar-heating system, it is called passive.

• A greenhouse has a clear roof that lets sunlight shine in, but won't let rising heat out.

• The process of making electricity from the sun's energy is called photovoltaics.

SOLAR ENERGY AND SPACE EXPLORATION

Solar energy is an important part of the space program.

The first earth-orbiting satellite launched by the United States in 1958 used solar cells to provide electricity to power its radios.

Apollo 11 astronaut erects a solar wind sheet
designed to collect atomic particles from the sun.

When astronauts went to
the moon, they left solar-
powered equipment there
to send scientific
information back to earth.

Six wings (solar battery panels) provided all the electricity for the *Skylab* space station.

Skylab used solar electricity to power its important equipment.

In fact, the *Skylab's* photovoltaic system was so huge that it could produce four thousand watts of electricity from the sun!

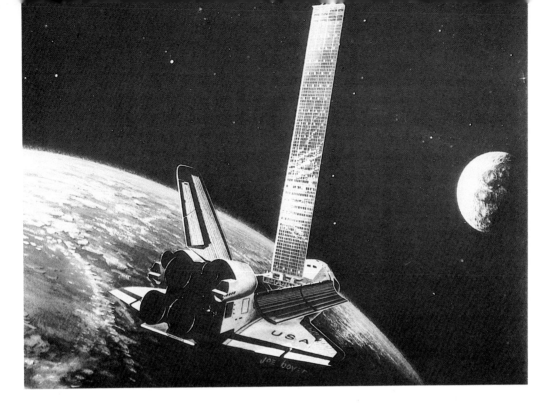

The space shuttles also use solar power to supply much of their electrical needs. And as the space shuttle missions become longer and longer, solar electricity will become more and more important.

Someday, we will have orbiting space colonies. These cities in space will count on the sun to supply most of their electricity and heat.

Some scientists believe that the sun's energy might someday be collected in huge orbiting solar panels. Then this energy could be beamed back and used on earth.

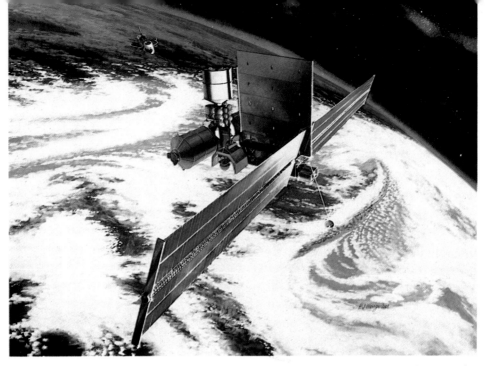

Future space stations, powered by solar panels, will provide scientific information.

Just as life on earth would not exist without the warmth and light of the sun, the space program could not have grown nearly as fast as it has without the help of solar electricity.

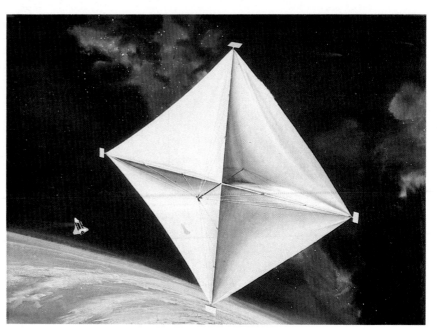

When Halley's comet returns in 1986, scientists hope to greet it with the Yankee Clipper, a 700-meter-square solar sail. The sail (thin aluminized plastic) will capture energy from the sun and power an attached spacecraft to fly formation with, study, and photograph the speeding comet.

SOLAR SAILING

Think about a sailboat. The large sail catches the wind, and the boat is pushed along.

Scientists are now working on a solar sail for powering spaceships.

Because there is no wind in space, these sailing spaceships will be pushed along by energy from the sun.

The sun radiates energy in many forms, some invisible to us. One form of energy is called "solar wind." This wind is actually made of high energy atomic and subatomic particles streaming away from the sun. These particles are so small and are moving so fast that they just pass through most objects.

Sunlight, another form of energy, is made up of "packets" of energy called photons. These photons push very slightly on all things that are in sunlight.

This pressure of sunlight is very weak, but since there is no friction in space, it is strong enough to push against a large sail and move a spaceship along.

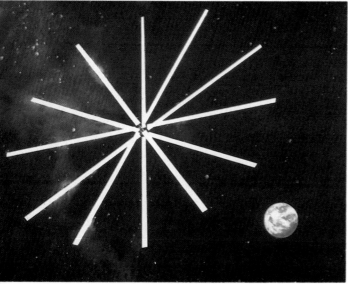

Artist's drawing shows
solar sail on
its way to
rendezvous with
an asteroid.

Besides the square solar sail these
spinning solar sails are also
being studied for a possible space
mission. Its twelve long sails
are powered by the sun's energy.

Solar sailing is one of
the most exciting hopes
for the future of the space
program. Using solar wind,
a spaceship could sail
through space almost
forever without needing to
refuel.

WORDS YOU SHOULD KNOW

absorptive(ab • ZORP • tiv) — capable of absorbing the sun's energy in the form of heat. Dull black is the most absorptive color.

active solar(AK • tiv SOH • ler) — a solar heating system that uses mechanical devices

greenhouse(GREEN • howss) — a building with a clear roof made of glass, plastic, or fiberglass. A greenhouse lets sunshine in, but won't let heat out.

passive solar(PASS • iv SOH • ler) — a solar heating system that uses no mechanical devices

photovoltaics(FOHT • oh • vahl • TAY • iks) — a process that converts sunlight into electricity

reflective(ri • FLEK • tiv) — capable of reflecting; does not absorb the sun's heat well, and thus stays cooler. Shiny, light colors are the most reflective.

silicon(SILL • ih • kon) — a mineral found in sand. After special treatment, silicon can convert sunlight into electricity. Silicon is used to make photovoltaic cells.

solar(SOH • ler) — from a Latin word that means sun

solar collector(SOH • ler kuh • LEK • ter) — a large black box or panel used to "collect" the sun's heat

INDEX

About the author

David Petersen has been a Marine Corps aviator, a magazine editor, a college teacher, and a free-lance writer, editor, and photographer. He is currently an associate editor for The Mother Earth News, *in Hendersonville, North Carolina.* Solar Energy at Work *is his sixth True Book.*

DATE DUE